A Little
Scana...
Cookbook

Janet Laurence

ILLUSTRATED BY AGNETHA PETERSEN

First published in the United States in 1990 by
Chronicle Books, 275 Fifth Street,
San Francisco, CA 94103.

ISBN 0-87701-743-3

9 8 7 6 5 4 3 2 1

Acknowledgement

I would like to thank my mother, Ruth Duffell, Mrs Bibi
Austin of Sweden, and all my Swedish relatives for their
help with this book, also Gerd Kirste and Truda Pendry
from Norway and Mr and Mrs Gunnar Henriksen from
Denmark, together with many friends who have given me
hospitality on visits to Scandinavia over the years,
providing wonderful meals and happy occasions.

Introduction

Rocky coastlines teeming with fish, long winters and short summers when the sun hardly sets, the Scandinavian countries have many factors in common, including a love of food that has led to much swapping of dishes. But though so much geography, history and culture is shared, there are also differences. Denmark is a lowland country which has made a major industry out of dairy and pig farming. Cream, butter, pork and bacon not only earn foreign currency but underpin the national cuisine. Norway is a mountainous land with deep fjords giving access to and dependence on the sea for much of its population. The cuisine is a simple one using a limited range of ingredients that are sparkling fresh and full of flavour. Sweden, land of forests and lakes with an indented coastline fringed with islands, has the most sophisticated cuisine. But though national dishes exist, many recipes are truly Scandinavian. Those included here give some idea of the richness and variety available. I have omitted game, reindeer and eel, all very popular in Norway and Sweden but often unobtainable elsewhere; the remaining ingredients should not prove too difficult to find.

Note All recipes are for four people unless otherwise stated.

Danish Liver Pâté

Light and smooth liver pâté is popular all over Scandinavia and it is often eaten for breakfast, especially in Norway. The Danish version is perhaps the smoothest of all, and full of flavor.

---

1 lb pork liver, minced
6 oz back pork fat, minced
5 fillets Scandinavian or 7 fillets Portuguese anchovies
2 small onions, peeled and chopped
2 tsp salt, freshly ground black pepper, pinch sugar
pinch allspice, pinch ground cloves
10 tbsp butter
scant 1½ cups flour
2½ cups milk
2 eggs, lightly beaten
(serves 12-15)

Blend the liver, fat, anchovies and onion to a smooth mixture, removing lumps and strings. Season well. Melt butter in a pan, add flour and stir over gentle heat for a few minutes then add milk gradually to make a smooth sauce. Add liver mixture and eggs, blending well. Pour into two 5-cup loaf pans (or one larger pan) lined with a double thickness of buttered foil. Place both pans in a roasting pan, add hot water to half the depth of the pâté and bake for about two hours at 325°F until the pâté is firm to the touch and an inserted skewer emerges clean. Turn out when cool.

Pytt i Panna

This Swedish hash is extremely popular in Denmark and Norway too. It is important that all the ingredients are carefully diced small and to the same size and cooked separately. Instead of a fried egg, a raw egg yolk in half a shell can be placed on top of each serving.

---

2 tbsp butter
2 tbsp oil
6 medium potatoes, boiled and cut into ¼-inch dice
2 medium onions, cut into ¼-inch dice
4-5 cups cooked meat (lamb or beef, with some ham or
uncooked bacon), cut into ¼-inch dice
salt and freshly ground black pepper
1 tbsp freshly chopped parsley
4-6 fried eggs (or 4-6 raw egg yolks)

Heat half the butter and oil and gently fry the potato dice until crisp and golden. Remove and keep warm. Heat remaining butter and oil, add onion and cook until transparent but not brown. Add the diced meats, increase heat slightly and cook, stirring constantly, until meat is browned on all sides and thoroughly reheated. Add the cooked potatoes, stirring gently until completely mixed. Season to taste. Add parsley. Serve with the fried eggs, or egg yolks in half an egg shell, on top.

Open Sandwiches

Open sandwiches are popular all over Scandinavia but the Danes have raised them to a fine art. Soft or hard bread of any variety can be used, the topping so generous no bread shows; the skill comes in selecting tasty ingredients that will complement or contrast with each other and then arranging them to make a visually satisfying snack. One or two sandwiches will do for lunch, or allow four per person for a main meal. Butter keeps the bread from getting soggy – Danes usually use a generous amount of unsalted butter or lard or pan drippings. Prepare the ingredients then assemble the sandwiches as near to eating time as possible. Cover with a damp cloth if not serving immediately. The sandwiches are eaten with a knife and fork. Here are a few popular suggestions:

Prawn Salad
Cram as many prawns or shrimps as possible all lined up in the same direction, rounded side up, on buttered white or sourdough bread; squeeze over lemon juice and season with freshly ground pepper. A sandwich of several layers is known as **The Rush Hour.**

Smoked Salmon with Scrambled Egg
Slices of smoked salmon on buttered white or rye bread, seasoned with a squeeze of lemon and freshly ground pepper then topped with a diagonal line of lightly scrambled egg garnished with a little fresh dill or asparagus tips.

Roast Beef and Potato Salad
Slices of rare roast beef on buttered rye or white bread topped with potato salad garnished with chopped chives and maybe a slice of tomato. A delicious variation replaces the potato salad with Danish caviar.

Chicken with Liverpaste
Spread homemade liver pâté or tinned pâté de foie gras on

buttered rye bread, top with sliced roast chicken and garnish with sliced tomato or parsley.

Cheese
Arrange thin slices of cheese–curled over looks good – on buttered bread and top with chopped or grated radish, sliced cucumber with a dusting of paprika, or halved grapes.

Potato and Salami
A Danish friend calls this 'the best sandwich in the world'. Use buttered rye bread. Add a layer of finely sliced boiled potato (new are best), then a layer of salami, pressing the ingredients down well. Garnish with chopped chives plus, if the occasion is very special, a raw egg yolk.

Oven Omelette

A popular, quick dish that can serve for lunch, supper or a snack.

---

4 eggs, lightly beaten
salt and freshly ground black pepper
1 ¼ cups light cream
generous 1 cup diced ham, preferably smoked
1 tbsp chopped chives

Season eggs, blend in cream, and add ham and chives, stirring well. Pour mixture into well-buttered round flameproof dish about 8 inches in diameter. Bake in a preheated oven at 350°F for about 25 minutes, until set and golden brown.

The same mixture (without the ham and chives) is often baked or cooked on top of the stove rather like a French omelette, and then served topped with small fried mackerel or fillets of smoked buckling arranged in a star shape then topped with chopped dill or chives served straight from the pan. Or it may be served with a creamy mushroom, lobster or sweetbread sauce. Sometimes the omelette is folded over this filling.

Swedish Yellow Pea Soup

By burying, drying, salting and pickling, the Scandinavians preserve as many foods as possible for the long winters. Amongst the dried foods they use is a round yellow pea that makes a superb soup; each country has its own version, usually cooked with salted pork or ham to add flavour. In Sweden the meat is cut into small pieces and forms part of the soup rather than being removed and eaten separately. Outside Scandinavia, these peas are sometimes available in delicatessens; ordinary split peas can be used but are a little different.

scant 2 cups dried yellow peas	*1 lb lightly salted salt pork or*
7½ cups water	*fresh pork shoulder, diced*
½ tsp salt, freshly ground	*or sliced*
black pepper	*½ tsp ground ginger*
1 onion	

Rinse peas and soak in water for about 12 hours then bring to the boil with the salt, pepper and onion. Simmer until soft, 1½-2 hours. Add the pork (soak it for about 12 hours if very salty and drain before adding) and ground ginger, and continue simmering until meat is cooked and tender. Remove the onion, check seasoning and serve.

Norwegian Lamb and Cabbage Casserole

The cold table appears on festive occasions. Pickled herrings, fish and meat dishes with varied accompaniments are arranged with style on a beautifully decorated table, a perfect way to entertain. The Swedish Smörgåsbord is the most elaborate and includes a number of hot dishes, but in Norway and Denmark there will seldom be more than one. This traditional lamb casserole could appear as part of a Norwegian Kolde Bord. When eating it look out for the whole peppercorns, or wrap them in cheesecloth and remove before serving.

2-2½ lb shoulder or lean breast of lamb, boneless,
cut into large cubes
1 small white cabbage, trimmed of stalk and sliced
1 tsp salt, 15 black peppercorns
1 bay leaf
about 2 cups water or light stock
finely chopped parsley

Blanch meat in boiling water for 2-3 minutes then drain. Layer cabbage and meat in a casserole dish, seasoning with salt and peppercorns. Add the bay leaf on top and enough stock to cover. Bring to the boil, skim, cover and cook very gently on top of stove or in a preheated oven at 350°F for about 1½ hours. Serve sprinkled with chopped parsley. Boiled or creamed potatoes go well and dark rye bread is a traditional accompaniment.

West Coast Salad

This is a favourite Scandinavian salad, a luscious mixture of shellfish caught on the western coasts and crisp lettuce, mushrooms and other salad stuffs. It appears on all great-occasion cold tables, the shellfish chosen according to availability and taste. Alas, these days fresh shellfish is scarce and prohibitively expensive, so frozen or canned is more commonly used.

---

1 crisp lettuce, shredded
1 cooked lobster, or 1 can of lobster meat, cut in serving pieces
15 cooked mussels, shelled, or 1 can mussels in brine, drained
½ cup cooked, peeled shrimps or prawns
1½ cups raw, sliced mushrooms, sprinkled with
juice of ½ lemon
2 tomatoes, peeled and quartered
1 cup cooked fresh or canned asparagus (2-inch pieces)
sprigs of dill

Dressing
1 clove garlic, crushed   salt and freshly ground
(optional)   black pepper
2 tbsp white wine vinegar   pinch sugar
6-8 tbsp olive oil
(serves 4-6)

Chill all the salad ingredients well, then layer in a bowl. Mix the dressing well, and toss the salad in it. Serve immediately garnished with sprigs of dill.

Cucumber Salad

This is an essential element of the cold table and a universal accompaniment throughout Scandinavia to meat and fish dishes. The sweet – sour flavour is very typical and the salad is known as 'Pickled Cucumber'. If the skin is tough, the cucumber should be peeled. Otherwise the skin can be left on or scored down its length with a fork or knife.

1 cucumber	2-3 tbsp sugar
salt	freshly ground black or
7 tbsp freshly squeezed lemon	white pepper
juice or white wine vinegar	2 tbsp freshly chopped
7 tbsp water	parsley

Slice cucumber very thinly, salt and leave to drain in a colander topped with a saucer plus a weight for 1-2 hours. Rinse off salt and squeeze the cucumber dry. Mix the lemon juice or vinegar, measured water, sugar to taste, pepper and a pinch of salt, stirring well to dissolve sugar. Pour the dressing over the cucumber.

Pickled Beets

Lightly pickled sweet-sour beets accompany a wide variety of foods throughout Scandinavia, particularly pork dishes and almost always appear on the cold table. This recipe is meant for swift consumption.

½ cup white wine vinegar
generous ½ cup water
½ cup sugar
I tsp salt
freshly ground black pepper
about 2 cups cooked, peeled and thinly sliced small beets
few cloves or I tsp caraway seeds (optional)
small piece horseradish (optional)

Bring the vinegar, water, sugar, salt and pepper to the boil in a stainless steel or enamelled saucepan and simmer for 2 minutes. Place the sliced beets in sterilised jars or a bowl and pour the hot marinade over it, adding cloves or caraway seeds as desired. A small piece of horseradish in each jar is said to help prevent mould forming. Keep the pickle in a cool place for at least 24 hours and up to 3 weeks before using.

Gravad Lax

The Norwegians and Swedes originally buried salmon as a me
preservation, using pine twigs or Scandinavia's favourite herb,
for flavouring. This recipe can also be used for trout or mackerel.
trout or mackerel will be ready in 24 hours, salmon will take 36-46
hours. Choose the middle cut of salmon or whole fat fish of the
smaller varieties. Most Scandinavians use rather more salt than
sugar but I prefer the slightly sweeter result given by equal
quantities.

---

1 middle cut of salmon or 1½-3½ lb trout or mackerel
For each 1 lb of prepared fish take:
1 tbsp coarse sea salt
1 tbsp sugar
1 tsp white peppercorns, crushed
large handful fresh dill

Scrape scales off the fish with back of knife, remove head and tail
and fillet if necessary, taking care not to tear flesh. Leave the skin
on. Avoid washing fish, instead wipe it with damp kitchen paper.
Mix together the salt, sugar and peppercorns. Select a shallow dish
as near the size of the salmon as possible. Place a layer of dill in
bottom. Cut salmon into two pieces and place one skin side down,
on the dill. Rub one third of the salt mixture into the flesh then add
a layer of dill. Rub another one third of salt mixture into the flesh of
second piece of salmon and place on top of first piece, matching
thin side to thick so fish makes as even-sized a parcel as possible.
Rub the last one third of salt mixture into the top skin and add
more dill (it's not possible to use too much). Cover with foil,
tucked over sides of dish. Place a small board on top and weight it
down. Leave in cool larder or fridge for 36 to 48 hours depending
on the thickness of fish and your personal taste. Then scrape off all

move any remaining bones, then slice as for smoked
_k slices are traditional. Serve garnished with lemon and
and accompanied by dill sauce.

Norwegian Fish Mousse

This is a favourite fish dish in Scandinavia.

3 lb whole fish, hake, cod, etc., with skin and bones,
to yield 1 lb when filleted and skinned
fine, dry breadcrumbs
1 fillet Swedish or 2 fillets Portuguese anchovies
4 tbsp butter
5 tbsp flour (or cornstarch)
1 1/4 cups light cream
2 eggs
2/3 cup heavy cream
2 tsp salt
1/4 tsp white pepper

Clean the fish and use skin and bone to make stock for prawn
sauce. Butter well a 6-7 cup ring mould or loaf pan and coat it
evenly with dried breadcrumbs. Blend the fillets with the anchovy,
butter and flour, and some of the cream if necessary, to a fine
purée. Place this in a bowl, season lightly, beat in eggs one at a time
and gradually add the cream, beating vigorously. Beat in remaining
seasonings. (If the mixture separates, put the bowl in warm water
for a few minutes whilst beating the mixture hard and it should
reconstitute itself.) Cook a trial piece of mousse in salted water. If
it is too loose, add a little more flour or whipped egg white. If it is
too stiff, add more liquid. When satisfactory, pour it into the
prepared pan. Bang the pan a couple of times on the table to
remove air pockets. Cover it with buttered foil, sealing tightly

around edges of pan. Place in a roasting pan filled with hot water to half the depth of the mould. Cook in preheated oven at 400°F for 1-1½ hours, until pudding is firm and an inserted skewer emerges clean. The water should not boil. Remove from oven and leave for five minutes before draining off any liquid and turning it out. Serve with prawn sauce.

Dill Sauce · Prawn Sauce

Dill Sauce This traditional accompaniment to pickled salmon is also good with other fish. Its flavour depends largely on using sweet Swedish mustard. If this is unavailable, substitute German mustard and a little extra sugar.

---

2 tsp sweet Swedish mustard
2 tsp superfine sugar
1 ½ tbsp white wine vinegar
⅔ cup light olive oil
1-2 tbsp chopped fresh dill
salt and freshly ground black pepper

Ensure that all ingredients are at room temperature. Place mustard, sugar and vinegar in a shallow bowl and mix well. Using a small whisk or wooden spoon, gradually blend in oil. Season to taste. Add the chopped dill. The sauce can be made with 1 tablespoon dried dill: allow to stand for several hours to allow the flavour to develop.

Prawn Sauce
2 tbsp butter   2 tbsp flour
⅔ cup good fish stock
⅔ cup light cream or extra-rich milk
salt and freshly ground black pepper
tomato purée
½-1 cup cooked, peeled prawns or shrimps, chopped

---

elt butter, add flour, and cook very gently for 2-3 minutes
without colouring. Add the liquid ingredients gradually to make a
smooth sauce. Season and add a little tomato purée to taste.
Simmer very gently for 10 minutes then adjust seasoning. The sauce
can be sharpened with a dash of tarragon wine vinegar. Just before
serving, add prawns or shrimps and heat them through for a
moment or two. Do not allow them to cook or they will
toughen.

Spiced Herring

Silver herrings dressed in a variety of spices and sweet sauces are an
essential element of the cold table. This traditional recipe is easy
and produces a delicious and unusual result.

2 lb very fresh herrings	2 tbsp allspice, crushed
4½ cups water	2 tbsp white peppercorns,
4 tbsp white wine vinegar	crushed
4 tbsp sea salt	10-15 bay leaves
2 cups fine brown sugar	
(serves 4-6 as a starter)	

Cut off the herrings' heads and tails and gut them. Wash and drain
well. Add vinegar to water, place herrings in a dish and cover
completely with liquid. Leave in a cool place for 24 hours, then
remove fish, rinse and drain well.

Mix together the salt, sugar and spices. Place a layer of mixture at
the bottom of a deep, narrow lidded dish and add a few bay leaves.
Add a layer of fish with a little spice mixture inside each, then
sprinkle over a layer of spice mixture with bay leaves and repeat
until all the fish have been used. Cover with remaining spice
mixture and bay leaves. Cover with foil and a lid and leave in a cool
place for about 48 hours. Remove fish and wipe off any spices
clinging to them. Bone by placing fish with inside of backbone

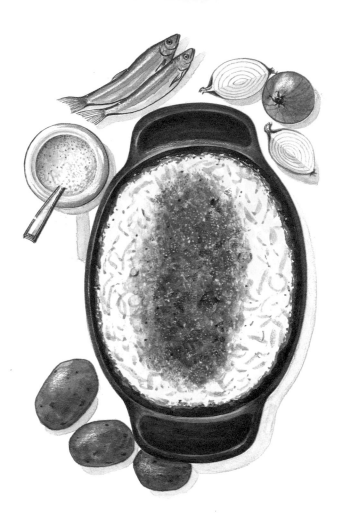

against a board and running a thumb along the outside of the spir
then ease backbone and other bones gently away from the flesh.
Check for any bones left behind and cut off the small fins. Cut fish
across in 1/2-inch slices.

Serve garnished with bay leaves and lemon. Either yoghurt or
sour cream mixed with plenty of chopped chives is a traditional
accompaniment. Rye or pumpernickel bread is also good. If using
for a main course, new potatoes, sliced hard-boiled eggs and beet
salad are traditional.

Jansson's Frestelse

Stories vary as to who Jansson (Johnson) was and why he had to be
tempted, but the dish is so good he could not have resisted its rich
delights. It should be made with mild Swedish anchovy fillets, but
Portuguese can be used if soaked first in milk for 1/2 hour. It is very
rich so watch what else is served in the meal.

---

2 large onions, sliced thinly   6 tbsp butter
5 medium-sized, white potatoes, boiled in their skins
16-18 Swedish anchovy fillets, bones removed or
2 cans good Portuguese anchovies, soaked in milk
toasted crumbs or crushed rusks
1 1/4 cups heavy cream
(serves 6 as a starter, 4 as a main course)

Cook onion gently in half the butter. Peel the potatoes and cut into
thick slices. Butter a medium-sized gratin dish very well. Arrange
half the potato on the bottom. Add the onions, then anchovies.
Cover with the remaining potato. If using Swedish anchovies pour a
little of the can's juices over the potato. Add enough cream just to
cover the potatoes. Sprinkle with crumbs and dot with butter.
Place in a preheated oven at 375°F for about 30 minutes, until
bubbling hot and browned. Serve immediately.

Swedish Meatballs

Every Scandinavian housewife has her own recipe for meatballs and there are also national variations. Swedes mix several meats and add soaked breadcrumbs for extra lightness. The Danes often form the mixture into oblongs instead of balls. The Norwegians usually use only beef and after browning finish cooking them in milk. When meatballs form part of the cold table, they are usually served without a sauce and can be either hot or cold.

---

1 large onion, very finely chopped
2 tbsp butter
9 tbsp breadcrumbs
⅔ cup mixed cream and soda water
1½ lb minced meat (about 1 lb chuck, braising or rump steak
and ½ lb veal or pork)
1 egg, lightly beaten
salt, pepper, pinch each ground cloves, ground allspice and
freshly grated nutmeg
lard or butter and oil for frying
(serves 4-6)

Cook onion in butter until soft. Leave to cool. Soak breadcrumbs in the cream and soda water. Mince meat several times or process it, then beat well with the onion and egg. Add the breadcrumbs, cream and soda water, beating until smooth. Fry a small portion to test seasoning. Using wet hands, form balls and fry them over a medium heat, shaking pan and turning balls to keep their shape. For a main course, make a sauce with the pan juices, or serve the meatballs with a mushroom sauce.

Pork with Prunes

Prunes are very popular in Scandinavia. Here they are used with apples to offset the richness of pork. This recipe is for loin, but fillet or tenderloin of pork can also be used, and takes much less time to cook. For a more economical dish, use boned lean spareribs or side pork.

---

4 lb boned loin of pork, middle cut
salt and freshly ground black pepper
10-12 prunes, ready-to-eat or soaked and stoned
1-2 tart apples, peeled, cored and sliced or diced
1 tbsp each butter and oil
2 cups dry white wine
1 cup heavy cream
1 tbsp redcurrant jelly
(serves 6)

Remove skin and fat from surface of meat. With a sharp knife make a deep slit parallel to the flap made by the removal of the bone. Season the inside of the meat and stuff with the fruit. Tie up the joint. Heat the butter and oil in a flameproof casserole. Seal and brown meat on all sides. Drain off fat, add wine and bring to boil. Season meat, cover with lid or foil and place in preheated oven at 325°F for about 3 hours until tender. Remove and keep warm. Skim off fat, add cream and redcurrant jelly to juices and gently bring to boil, stirring all the time, until sauce is smooth. Simmer for 2-3 minutes, check seasoning and serve with the meat. The joint is also very good cold.

Sailor's Stew

Most Scandinavians love the sea and many who live away from the water have holiday homes with a small boat on the coast, by a lake or on one of the innumerable small islands. This rib-warming stew is fit welcome for a hungry sailor.

---

1 1/4 - 1 3/4 lb steak, chuck, top round or rump,
cut in thick slices
4 tbsp butter
salt and freshly ground black pepper
2 cups thinly sliced onions
5-6 medium potatoes, sliced
about 3/4 cup water
2 1/2 cups beer
2 tbsp chopped parsley
diced cold butter

Pound meat lightly and brown in butter on both sides, over a high heat. Remove and season. Cook onions in same pan until soft. Line the bottom of a buttered casserole dish with half the potato then layer the meat and onions on top. Finish with remaining potato and season lightly. Add the water to the pan in which the meat and onions were cooked and bring to the boil, scraping in any bits stuck to the bottom. Simmer for a few minutes then pour it into the casserole. Add the beer, cover and cook in a preheated oven at 350°F for 1 1/2-2 hours. Sprinkle with parsley, dot with the knobs of cold butter and serve.

Hasselback Potatoes

Potatoes are a staple throughout Scandinavia. In Norway they are almost always boiled, in Denmark new potatoes are glazed, but the Swedes have devised this crisp and flavourful method of roasting.

8-12 medium potatoes, peeled	3 tbsp grated hard cheese
3 tbsp butter, melted	2 tbsp fine, toasted breadcrumbs
1 tsp salt	

Cut each potato not quite through, in a series of slices so that they are still joined together at the bottom. Roll them in the melted butter to coat then place in roasting pan with sliced side uppermost. Pour over any remaining butter. Sprinkle with salt and roast in hot oven, basting frequently, until half cooked, 30-40 minutes according to size of potato. Coat them with the mixed grated cheese and breadcrumbs and continue roasting without further basting until they are cooked through.

Red Cabbage

Cabbage is one of the few vegetables grown during the short Scandinavian summer. Red cabbage, piquant with apple and a touch of vinegar and sweetened with syrup or redcurrant jelly, is a traditional accompaniment to main dishes.

---

1 medium red cabbage
3 tbsp butter
1 medium onion, finely chopped
2 medium cooking apples, peeled, cored and sliced
2 tsp caraway seeds (optional)
salt and freshly ground black pepper
2 tbsp corn syrup or 4 tbsp redcurrant jelly
3 tbsp white wine vinegar
3 tbsp water
(serves 6-8)

Quarter the cabbage and discard tough stem, then slice each quarter very thinly. Melt butter in flameproof casserole dish, add cabbage, stir well and fry over moderate heat for about five minutes, stirring constantly. Season, add remaining ingredients, cover and cook very gently until cabbage is quite soft, approximately 1½-2 hours. Stir from time to time and add a little more water if dish begins to dry out. If using redcurrant jelly rather than syrup, stir this in about 30 minutes before the end of cooking. Check seasoning at end of cooking, adding a little more syrup or vinegar as necessary to achieve a balanced sweet-sour flavour. This dish improves with reheating.

Danish Apple Pudding

Apples grow well in northern Europe, the length of the summer days making up for spring's late start. They are the main ingredient used for a pudding that is a favourite throughout Scandinavia, each country offering a slightly different version. In Sweden the layered composition of fried crumbs and apple purée is cooked, making a dessert that can be unmoulded when cold. Norway layers the crumbs and apple with whipped cream sweetened with a little sugar (Norwegians always sweeten their cream for desserts this way). Perhaps the best version is this. Danish pudding, which uses fried rye or pumpernickel crumbs mixed with a little grated chocolate for layering with the cooked apple. Its name, Bondepige med Slor, means 'veiled country girl'. The 'veil' is the cream decorating the top.

---

2 lb cooking apples
3 tbsp water
sugar to taste
2 cups grated dark rye or pumpernickel breadcrumbs
½ cup butter
3 tbsp sugar
2 tbsp grated dark chocolate
⅔ cup whipped cream
grated dark chocolate for garnish

Peel, core and slice apples and gently cook with water until tender. Sweeten to taste and cool. Fry breadcrumbs in butter with 3 tablespoons sugar, stirring until crisp. Remove from heat and stir in grated chocolate and mix to melt. Cool. Layer crumbs and apple purée in a glass bowl, beginning and ending with crumbs. Decorate with whipped cream and extra grated chocolate. Chill before serving but eat within a few hours, before crumbs go soggy.

Wholewheat crumbs make a good substitute if rye or pumpernickel are unavailable.

Katrinplommonsuffle

This is another popular dish with prunes. It is a wonderful dish for entertaining since it can be prepared well in advance and is very impressive, as well as delicious.

---

8 oz prunes, cooked, stoned and chopped
4 large egg whites
¾ cup sugar
10 almonds, blanched and roughly chopped

Butter well a 6 cup flameproof dish (a flatter one than the usual round soufflé dish is good for this recipe). Whip egg whites to stiff peaks. One tablespoon at a time, whip in the sugar, fruit and almonds alternately. The mixture should be stiff and shiny. Spread mixture evenly into the dish. It can be refrigerated at this stage for several hours. Bake in a preheated oven at 350°F for about 30 minutes until soufflé is well risen and browned. Serve immediately. Oven heat can be increased up to 400°F, which will cut cooking time; the exact timing is governed by the shape of the dish – a shallow container, rather than the traditional round soufflé dish, can be very effective – and consequent depth of the mixture.

Red Fruit Pudding

This is the very best of all the many Scandinavian fruit soups, some sour and some sweet. Two or more red fruits are usually used but it can be made with just one. The consistency should be thick but not gelatinous. It is traditionally served with cream.

1½ lb soft red fruits (redcurrants, raspberries, strawberries, etc)
scant 2 cups water, or half water and half medium dry
white wine
about 1 cup sugar
pinch salt
3 tbsp water
3 tbsp potato flour, arrowroot powder or cornstarch
4 tbsp slivered almonds for garnish

Trim and clean the fruit, cutting large berries in half. Place in pan with water or water and wine, bring to boil and simmer, covered, until fruit is soft. Pass through a fine sieve. The yield should be approximately 2½ cups; if it is less, top up with a little water. Add sugar and salt and heat gently until the sugar has melted, then bring to boiling point. Check sweetness, adding a little more sugar if necessary. Blend the 3 tbsp water into the potato flour, arrowroot powder or cornstarch. Mix in a little boiling fruit juice then pour the mixture into the pan of juice. Simmer gently until the liquid has thickened, stirring constantly. Remove from heat. When slightly cooled pour the soup into a glass bowl, chill it and scatter slivered almonds over the top. Danes serve this pudding in individual bowls rinsed with cold water and sprinkled with sugar. More sugar is sprinkled over the top to prevent a skin forming, then the almonds are scattered on top.

Swedish Pancakes

These rich little pancakes are eaten all over Scandinavia. They are the traditional Thursday night pudding in Sweden after pea soup with pork. Scandinavians eat them with a semi-sweet preserve – the favourite is made with lingonberry (a close equivalent is cranberry sauce) – or with jam. They are always made very thin.

---

3 eggs
1 cup each of milk and light cream
scant 1 cup sifted flour
4 tbsp unsalted butter, melted
pinch salt
1 tbsp sugar
butter for frying
(serves 6-8)

Beat eggs well with half the milk and cream. Add flour and beat until smooth. Gradually stir in the remaining liquid, then the melted butter, salt and sugar. Heat a frying pan thoroughly, brushing it with a little butter for first pancake. Further buttering should not be necessary. Make thin, small pancakes (3 inches diameter). Cook each pancake over medium heat until surface bubbles and is set. Turn and cook briefly on other side until golden brown. Keep warm until all are ready. Serve immediately with lingonberry jam and cream if desired.

Danish Pastries

Viennese bakers brought the croissant to Copenhagen in the early nineteenth century. The Danes adored them and soon variations – improvements they would say – were being made that resulted in the sweet, light-as-air pastries now known throughout the world. Few Scandinavians bake their own – they can buy superb examples from their local pâtisserie. For those who would like to try, the secret is to have all ingredients (including flour) as cold as possible and to work in a cold room.

---

2 tbsp fresh yeast or active dry yeast
10 tbsp cold milk
¼ tsp salt
2 tbsp superfine sugar
1 egg
2½ cups flour
1¼ cups unsalted butter
Fillings
Butter cream (equal parts butter and confectioners' sugar), crème patissière, almond paste, jam, raisins and nuts; icing to finish

---

Crush fresh yeast in milk or mix dry yeast with flour. Mix sugar and salt with flour and make a basic bread dough with the milk mixed with egg. Do not knead or leave to rise but roll out immediately to a rectangle about ¼ inch thick and about 16 inch x 10 inch. In advance, beat the very cold butter to a rectangle sufficiently large almost to cover the two-thirds of the pastry nearest to you; the beating will make it pliable.

Place butter in position, then fold the pastry like a letter, making the first fold with the unbuttered portion so the buttered sides are separated. Seal the sides with the edge of your hand, and leave pastry in refrigerator to rest for 20 minutes. Repeat, rolling and folding five times and resting in between, giving pastry a quarter turn each time so that the open side is always at right angles to the working edge. Finally roll out the dough to initial thickness and cut for pastries.

Here are some of the most popular shapes.

Windmills Cut 4 inch squares, then cut from each corner almost to the middle and lift dough on right side of each cut to centre, pressing into place.

Spandau Place blob of jam, custard or almond paste in middle of each square, fold each corner into the centre and press down firmly.

Twisted Knots Cut dough into strips ¼ inch wide and 10 inches long. Press the ends of two strips together then twist the strips round each other, press the other ends together and wind into a circle with one end buried in the middle, the other tucked underneath.

Combs Cut out a roughly 12 inch square. Spread butter cream along the centre and cover it with the plain top and bottom thirds of the pastry as if folding a letter. Cut dough into 1½ inch slices and make a series of cuts along one side, halfway into filling.

Baking Once formed, leave the pastries on lightly buttered baking sheets in a warm room, covered, until they have doubled in size. Bake in preheated oven at 425°F until crisp and golden brown. Leave to cool slightly then glaze with confectioners' sugar icing and serve as quickly as possible. Do not mix different shapes on the same baking sheets as they may take different times to bake.

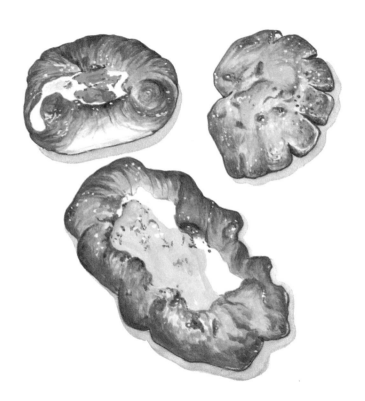

Finnish Biscuits

Of all the enticing Scandinavian biscuits baked at Christmas time, I have chosen these small logs: they are incredibly light and short but easy to make. Almond topped, they are known as Finnish Bread, though they are no daily diet there!

½ cup butter
¼ cup superfine sugar
I generous cup flour, sifted
I egg white, lightly beaten
10 almonds in their skins, chopped and mixed with
2 tbsp granulated sugar

Cream butter and sugar until very light and fluffy. Carefully fold the flour in then chill for an hour or so. Divide mixture in four and roll each part into a rope about ½ inch thick. Brush with lightly beaten egg white and cut into 2 inch lengths. Dip these into the almond and sugar mixture then place on a greased baking sheet. Bake in a preheated oven at 400°F for 10 minutes until lightly coloured. Cool on a rack then store in airtight tin.

Tosca Cake

Scandinavians love Tosca cake with its almond fudge topping. My mother makes the best I have ever tasted and this is her recipe.

---

2 large eggs
generous ½ cup superfine sugar
½ cup flour, sifted with 1½ tsp baking powder and pinch salt
4 tbsp butter, just melted

Topping
½ cup butter, softened
⅔ cup blanched almonds, lightly toasted and roughly chopped
½ cup superfine sugar
2 tbsp flour
2 tbsp cream or milk

Grease and line with parchment paper the bottom and sides of an 8-inch cake pan. Beat the eggs until thick and pale then gradually beat in the sugar until mixture falls in a thick ribbon. Fold in the flour mixture and the cooled melted butter. Bake in pan at 325°F for 30 minutes, or until the cake is nearly cooked. Meanwhile stir the topping ingredients together. Just before the cake is ready, heat the topping mixture, stirring constantly, allowing it to melt and come just to the boil. Remove cake from oven carefully and spread the topping over it. Place under a medium-hot broiler until topping is golden brown, watching that the sides of the cake don't burn. Cool the pan on a rack for about two hours, then carefully remove the cake.

Glögg · Rosehip Tea

Glögg is traditionally served on Christmas Eve, a warming drink for the coldest of northern nights. There are many variations. Some recipes omit wine, others add vermouth and/or white wine, and proportions and spices vary. Adapt this recipe to your taste and pocket. Without spirits the drink is a very good mulled wine rather than glögg.

---

1 bottle unflavored aquavit (or vodka)
1 bottle red wine, preferably Bordeaux
seeds of 10 cardamom pods
6 cloves
peel of an orange, preferably Seville, removed without pith
1 stick cinnamon
1½ cups raisins
1 cup superfine sugar
1 cup blanched almonds

Place everything except the almonds in a bowl, stir well, cover and leave to stand for about 12 hours. Heat gently, stirring to melt the sugar, to just below boiling point. Ignite the spirits, add the almonds and serve in small cups or punch glasses.

Traditionally lump sugar was used, placed on a wire grid, and the flaming glögg was spooned over again and again until the sugar had melted into the hot spiced spirit.

Rosehip Tea In autumn Scandinavians cull the woods and hedgerows for wild mushrooms and berries. Rosehips are made into a soup and this refreshing tea.

Bring a cup of water to the boil, add 3 tablespoons crushed, dried rosehips (or use rosehip juice) and simmer for 10 minutes. Remove from the heat and leave for a few minutes then strain into a cup and serve with sugar or a little honey.

Index

Apple Pudding, Danish 43

Beets, Pickled 20
Biscuits, Finnish 55

Cabbage, Red 40
Cucumber Salad 19

Danish Apple Pudding 43
Danish Liver Pâté 4
Danish Pastries 51
Dill Sauce 27

Finnish Biscuits 55
Fish Mousse, Norwegian 24

Glögg 59
Gravad Lax 23

Hasselback Potatoes 39
Herring, Spiced 28

Jansson's Frestelse 31

Katrinplommonsuffle 44

Liver Pâté, Danish 4

Meatballs, Swedish 32

Norwegian Fish Mousse 24
Norwegian Lamb and Cabbage
    Casserole 15

Open Sandwiches 8
Oven Omelette 11

Pancakes, Swedish 48
Pickled Beets 20
Pork with Prunes 35
Potatoes, Hasselback 39
Prawn Sauce 27
Pytt i Panna 7

Red Cabbage 40
Red Fruit Pudding 47
Rosehip Tea 59

Sailor's Stew 36
Salads: Cucumber 19
        West Coast 16
Sandwiches, Open 8
Sauces: Dill 27
        Prawn 27
Soup, Swedish Yellow Pea 12
Spiced Herring 28
Swedish Meatballs 32
Swedish Pancakes 48
Swedish Yellow Pea Soup 12

Tosca Cake 56

West Coast Salad 16